This book belongs to

_____

Dr. Markethia Mull @ mmull@maminomull.com

Noun...ABC's Activity Book/Solomon Mull
Noun...ABC's Activity Book/Dr. Markethia Mull

Printed in the United States of America/Houston, TX

ISBN **979-8-9853160-7-0**

Dear Parent(s),

One of my current capacities is tutoring, and I tutor many students in the fourth grade and beyond who lack the ability to define nouns, verbs, and adjectives. These students also cannot identify those parts of speech in isolation. I want to bridge this literacy gap. This activity book includes skills like letter/sound association, beginning sounds in isolation, writing, and tracing. Nouns are a focal point for the activity book. Are you wondering why an educator would create an activity book identifying nouns? Decades ago, Language Arts was taught as a single subject and not coupled with Reading. There was a time when the school schedule had 45 minutes to 60 minutes geared toward teaching an array of Language Arts skills. Fast forward to the current, Language Arts and Reading are combined as one where Reading is the main subject. So, how can students learn to construct a sentence? I plead with you to consider this helpful nugget. When your child is learning letter/sound association, you can extend the learning to alliteration (same letter or sound at the beginning of adjacent or closely connected words) and identifying nouns. Yes, you can wait for the teacher to introduce those parts of speech, but how in-depth will it be?

Respectfully,

Dr. M & Solomon

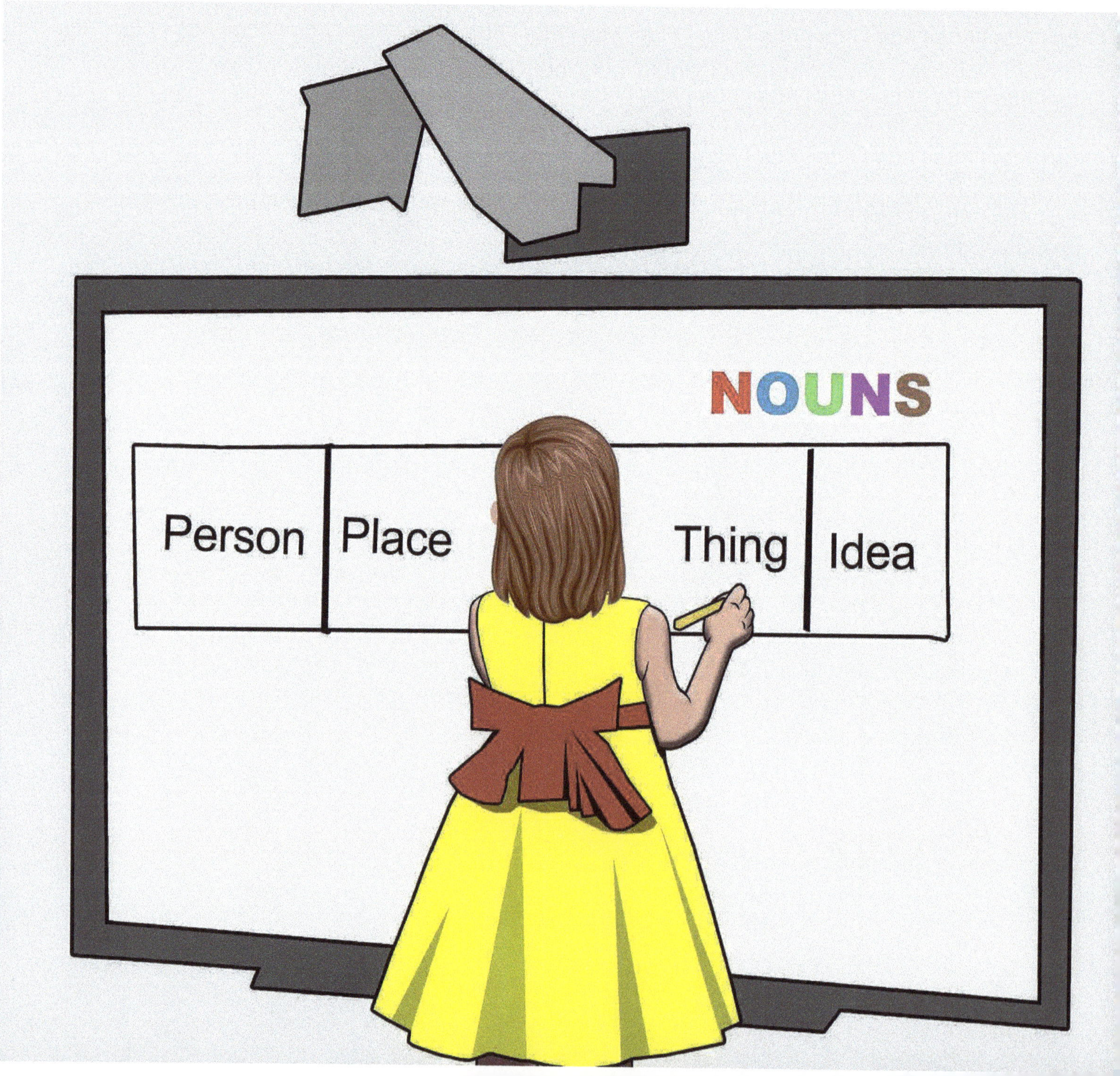
NOUNS
Person
Place
Thing
Idea

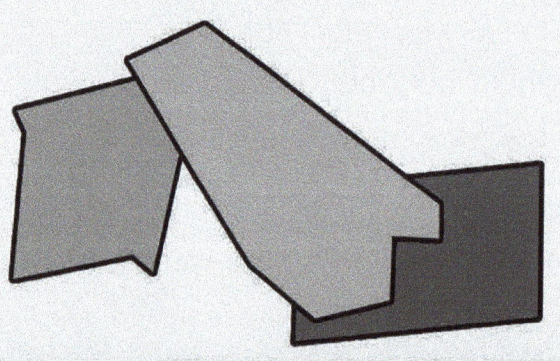

Directions: Say each word. Color each picture that starts with the letter Aa and is a noun. Cross (X) out each picture that does not begin with the letter or is not a noun. Use the box to draw a picture that starts with the letter and is a noun. Trace each letter at the bottom of the page.

Enrichment Activity

Directions: Look at the pictures and label the nouns only. Write the word that starts with the letter Aa and is a noun.

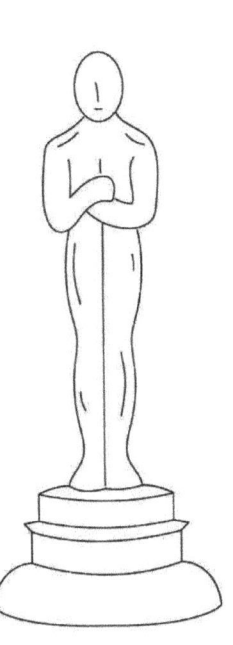

_____

_____

_____

_____

_____

Directions: Say each word. Color each picture that starts with the letter Bb and is a noun. Cross (X) out each picture that does not begin with the letter or is not a noun. Use the box to draw a picture that starts with the letter and is a noun. Trace each letter at the bottom of the page.

Enrichment Activity

Directions: Look at the pictures and label the nouns only. Write the word that starts with the letter Bb and is a noun.

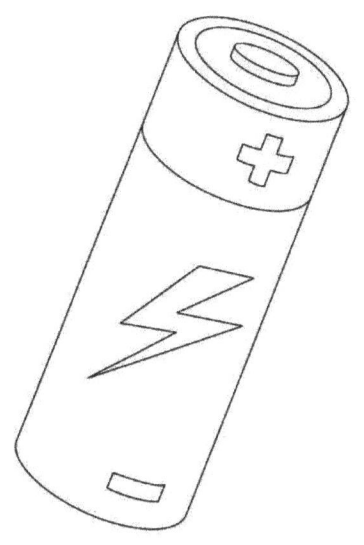

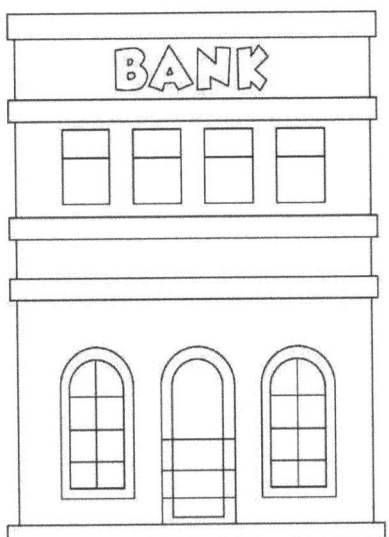

_____

_____

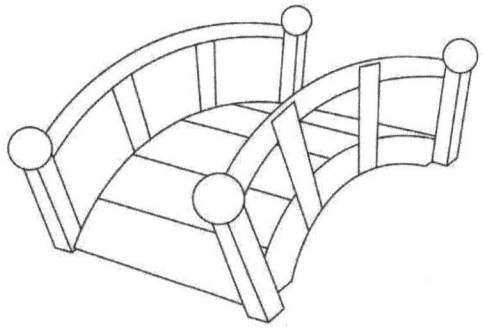

_____

_____

_____

Directions: Say each word. Color each picture that starts with the letter Cc and is a noun. Cross (X) out each picture that does not begin with the letter or is not a noun. Use the box to draw a picture that starts with the letter and is a noun. Trace each letter at the bottom of the page.

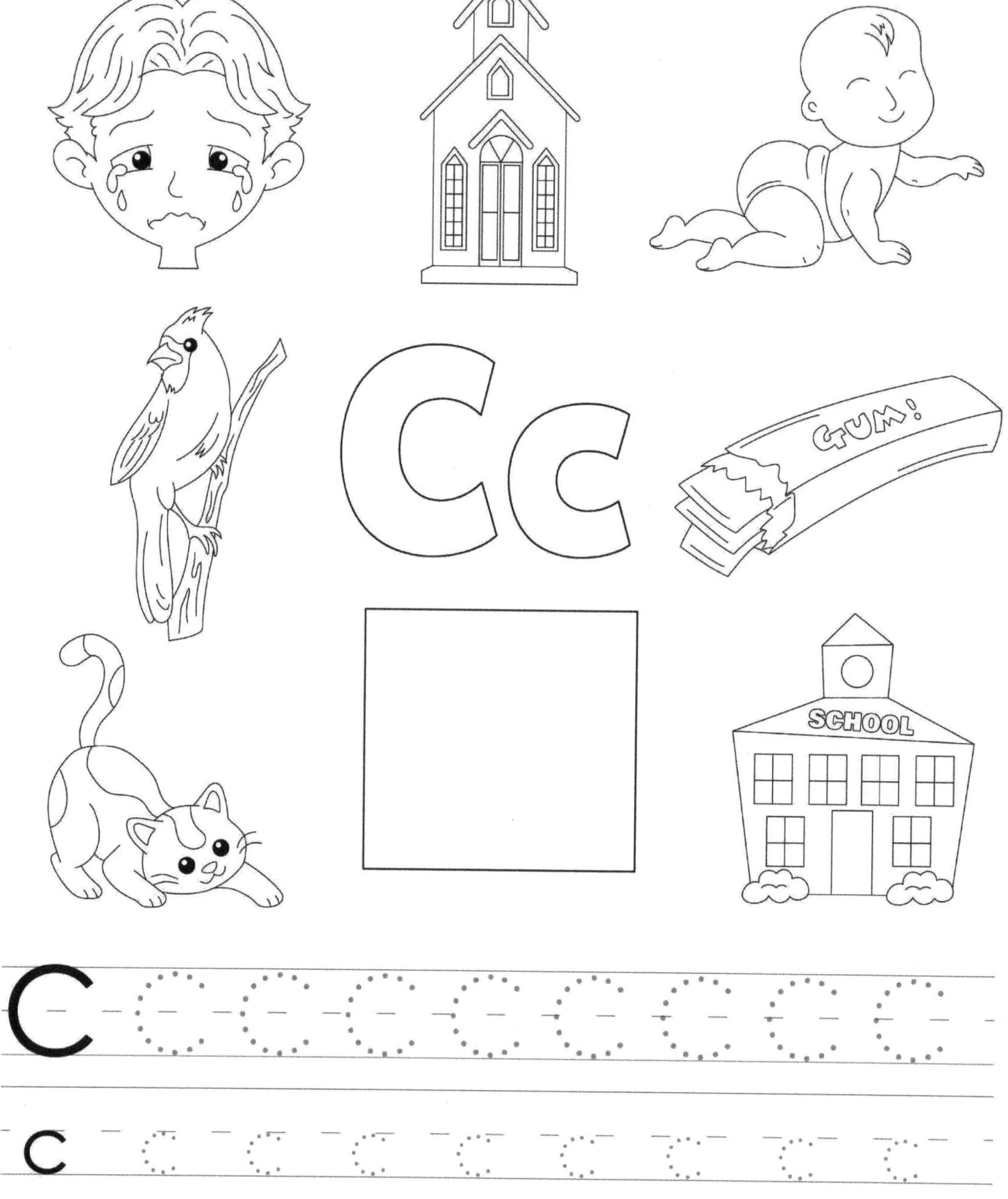

Enrichment Activity

Directions: Look at the pictures and label the nouns only. Write the word that starts with the letter Cc and is a noun.

_____

_____

_____

_____

_____

Directions: Say each word. Color each picture that starts with the letter Dd and is a noun. Cross (X) out each picture that does not begin with the letter or is not a noun. Use the box to draw a picture that starts with the letter and is a noun. Trace each letter at the bottom of the page.

Enrichment Activity

Directions: Look at the pictures and label the nouns only. Write the word that starts with the letter Dd and is a noun.

_____   _____

_____

_____   _____

Directions: Say each word. Color each picture that starts with the letter Ee and is a noun. Cross (X) out each picture that does not begin with the letter or is not a noun. Use the box to draw a picture that starts with the letter and is a noun. Trace each letter at the bottom of the page.

Enrichment Activity

Directions: Look at the pictures and label the nouns only. Write the word that starts with the letter Ee and is a noun.

Directions: Say each word. Color each picture that starts with the letter Ff and is a noun. Cross (X) out each picture that does not begin with the letter or is not a noun. Use the box to draw a picture that starts with the letter and is a noun. Trace each letter at the bottom of the page.

Enrichment Activity

Directions: Look at the pictures and label the nouns only. Write the word that starts with the letter Ff and is a noun.

_____   _____

_____

_____   _____

Directions: Say each word. Color each picture that starts with the letter Gg and is a noun. Cross (X) out each picture that does not begin with the letter or is not a noun. Use the box to draw a picture that starts with the letter and is a noun. Trace each letter at the bottom of the page.

Enrichment Activity

Directions: Look at the pictures and label the nouns only. Write the word that starts with the letter Gg and is a noun.

_____

_____

_____

_____

_____

Directions: Say each word. Color each picture that starts with the letter Hh and is a noun. Cross (X) out each picture that does not begin with the letter or is not a noun. Use the box to draw a picture that starts with the letter and is a noun. Trace each letter at the bottom of the page.

Enrichment Activity

Directions: Look at the pictures and label the nouns only. Write the word that starts with the letter Hh and is a noun.

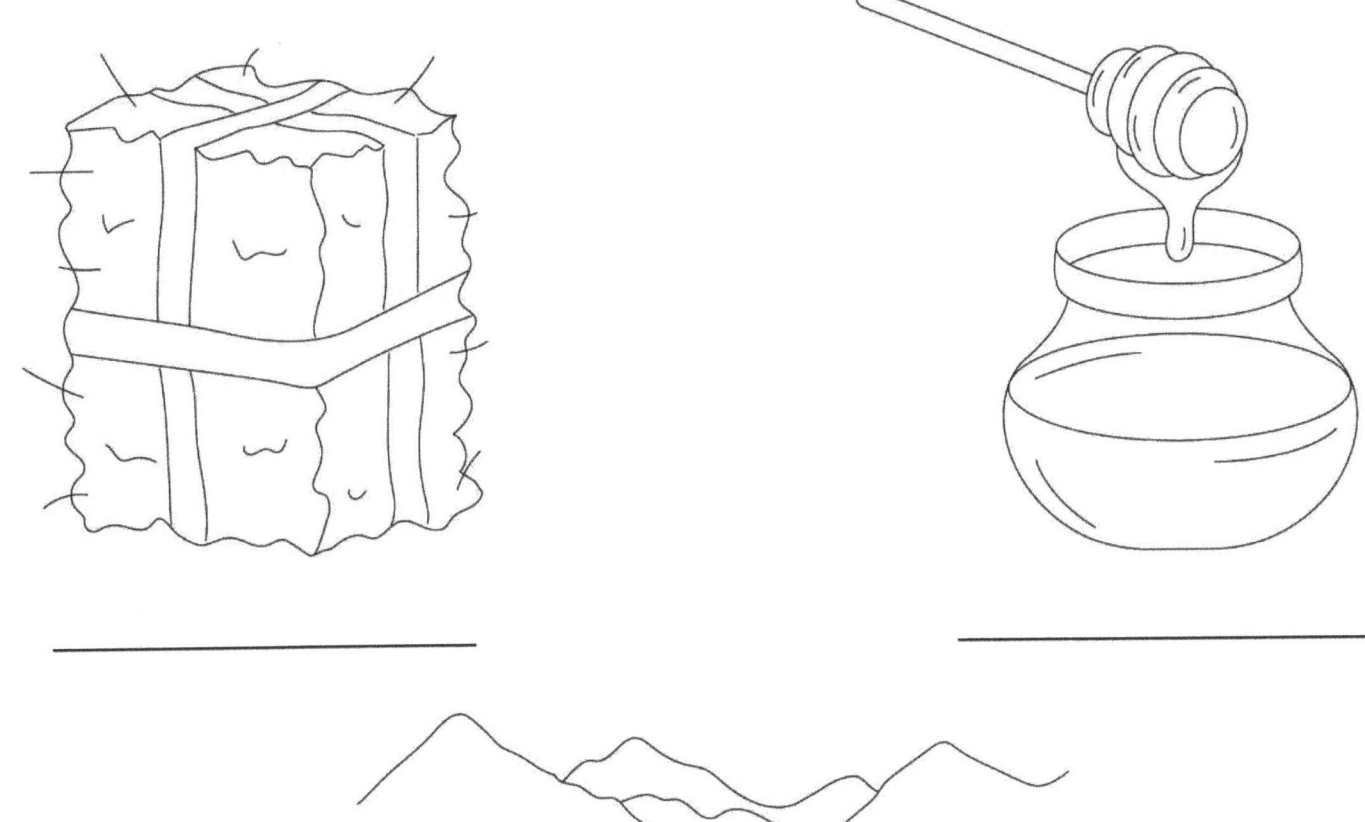

_____   _____

_____

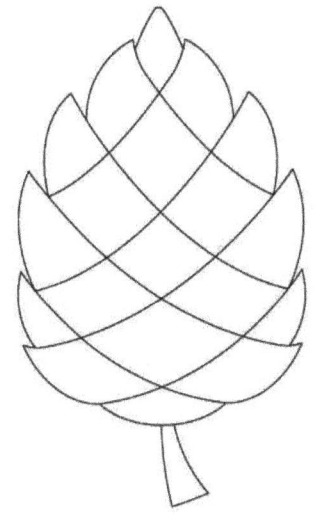

_____   _____

Directions: Say each word. Color each picture that starts with the letter Ii and is a noun. Cross (X) out each picture that does not begin with the letter or is not a noun. Use the box to draw a picture that starts with the letter and is a noun. Trace each letter at the bottom of the page.

Enrichment Activity

Directions: Look at the pictures and label the nouns only. Write the word that starts with the letter Ii and is a noun.

_____   _____

_____

_____   _____

Directions: Say each word. Color each picture that starts with the letter Jj and is a noun. Cross (X) out each picture that does not begin with the letter or is not a noun. Use the box to draw a picture that starts with the letter and is a noun. Trace each letter at the bottom of the page.

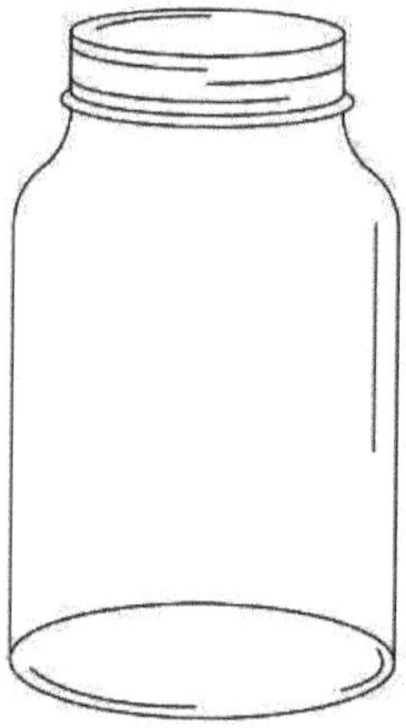

J _ _ J _ _ J _ _ J _ _ J _ _ J _ _ J _ _ J _ _ J

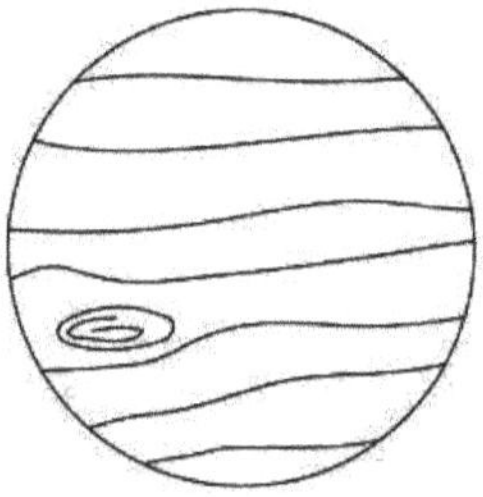

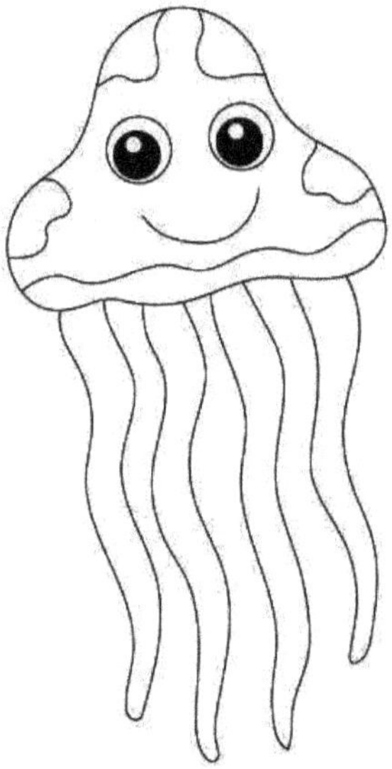

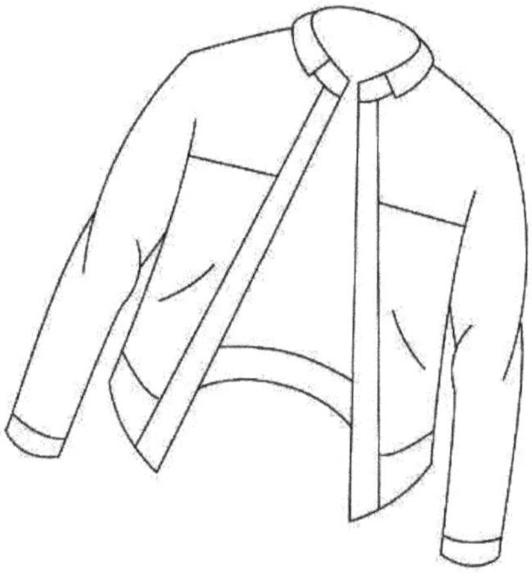

j _ _ j _ _ j _ _ j _ _ j _ _ j _ _ j _ _ j _ _ j

Enrichment Activity

Directions: Look at the pictures and label the nouns only. Write the word that starts with the letter Jj and is a noun.

Directions: Say each word. Color each picture that starts with the letter Kk and is a noun. Cross (X) out each picture that does not begin with the letter or is not a noun. Use the box to draw a picture that starts with the letter and is a noun. Trace each letter at the bottom of the page.

Enrichment Activity

Directions: Look at the pictures and label the nouns only. Write the word that starts with the letter Kk and is a noun.

_____

_____

_____

_____

_____

Directions: Say each word. Color each picture that starts with the letter Ll and is a noun. Cross (X) out each picture that does not begin with the letter or is not a noun. Use the box to draw a picture that starts with the letter and is a noun. Trace each letter at the bottom of the page.

L l

Enrichment Activity

Directions: Look at the pictures and label the nouns only. Write the word that starts with the letter Ll and is a noun.

_____

_____

_____

_____

_____

Directions: Say each word. Color each picture that starts with the letter Mm and is a noun. Cross (X) out each picture that does not begin with the letter or is not a noun. Use the box to draw a picture that starts with the letter and is a noun. Trace each letter at the bottom of the page.

$\pi = 3{,}14$

$(x+y)^2 - (x+y)^2$

Mm

M M M M M M M M M M

m m m m m m m m m m

Enrichment Activity

Directions: Look at the pictures and label the nouns only. Write the word that starts with the letter Mm and is a noun.

_____   _____

_____

_____   _____

Directions: Say each word. Color each picture that starts with the letter Nn and is a noun. Cross (X) out each picture that does not begin with the letter or is not a noun. Use the box to draw a picture that starts with the letter and is a noun. Trace each letter at the bottom of the page.

Enrichment Activity

Directions: Look at the pictures and label the nouns only. Write the word that starts with the letter Nn and is a noun.

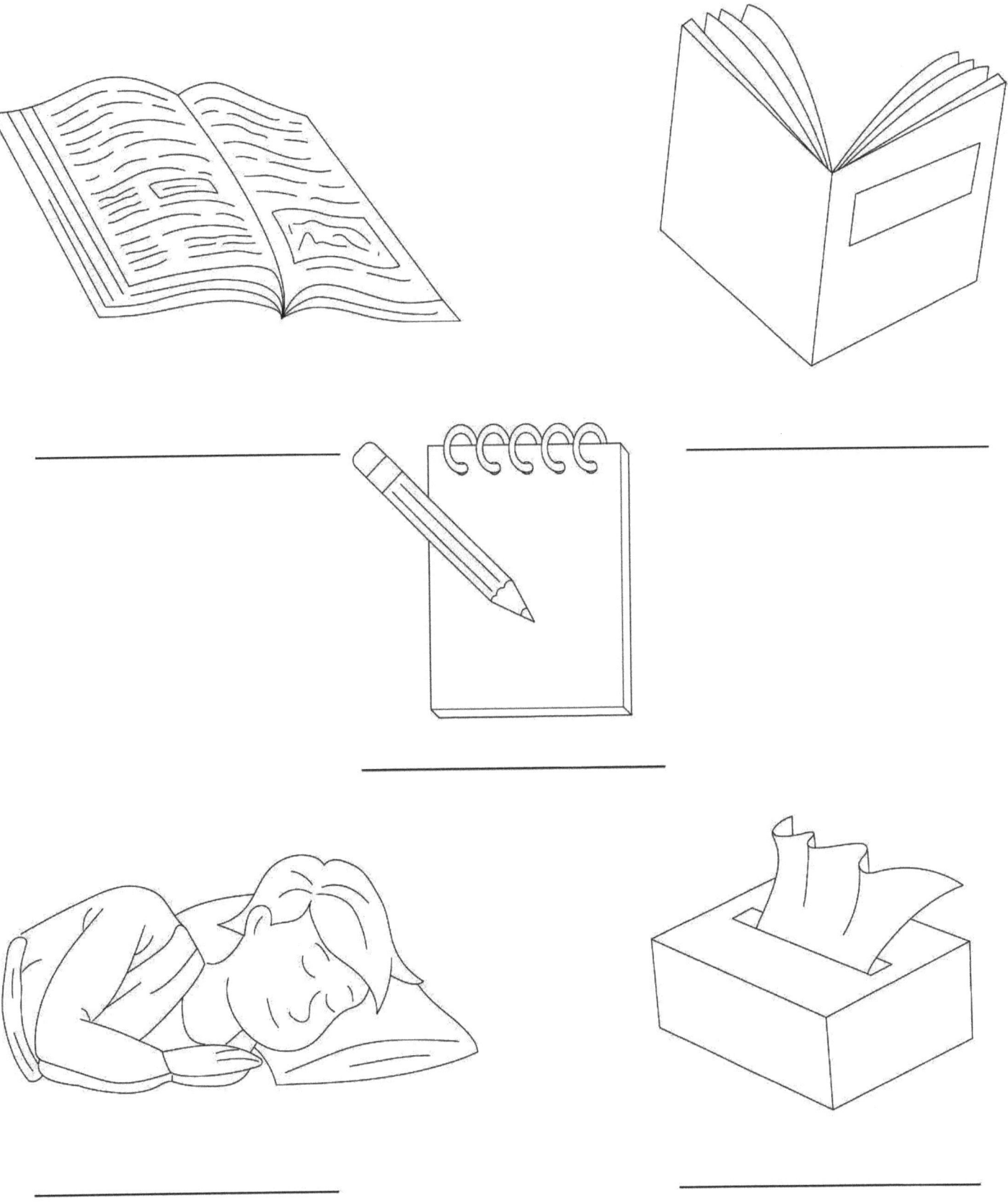

Directions: Say each word. Color each picture that starts with the letter Oo and is a noun. Cross (X) out each picture that does not begin with the letter or is not a noun. Use the box to draw a picture that starts with the letter and is a noun. Trace each letter at the bottom of the page.

Enrichment Activity

Directions: Look at the pictures and label the nouns only. Write the word that starts with the letter Oo and is a noun.

_____

_____

_____

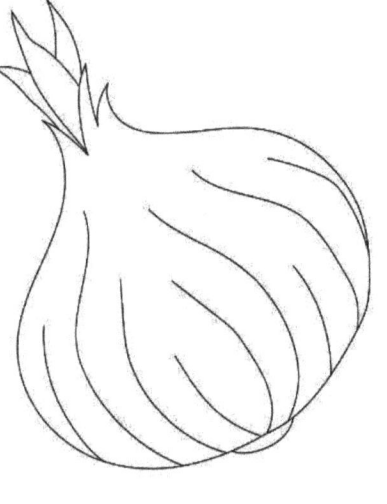

_____

_____

Directions: Say each word. Color each picture that starts with the letter Pp and is a noun. Cross (X) out each picture that does not begin with the letter or is not a noun. Use the box to draw a picture that starts with the letter and is a noun. Trace each letter at the bottom of the page.

Enrichment Activity

Directions: Look at the pictures and label the nouns only. Write the word that starts with the letter Pp and is a noun.

_____

_____

_____

_____

_____

Directions: Say each word. Color each picture that starts with the letter Qq and is a noun. Cross (X) out each picture that does not begin with the letter or is not a noun. Use the box to draw a picture that starts with the letter and is a noun. Trace each letter at the bottom of the page.

Enrichment Activity

Directions: Look at the pictures and label the nouns only. Write the word that starts with the letter Qq and is a noun.

_____   _____

_____

_____   _____

Directions: Say each word. Color each picture that starts with the letter Rr and is a noun. Cross (X) out each picture that does not begin with the letter or is not a noun. Use the box to draw a picture that starts with the letter and is a noun. Trace each letter at the bottom of the page.

Red

Enrichment Activity

Directions: Look at the pictures and label the nouns only. Write the word that starts with the letter Rr and is a noun.

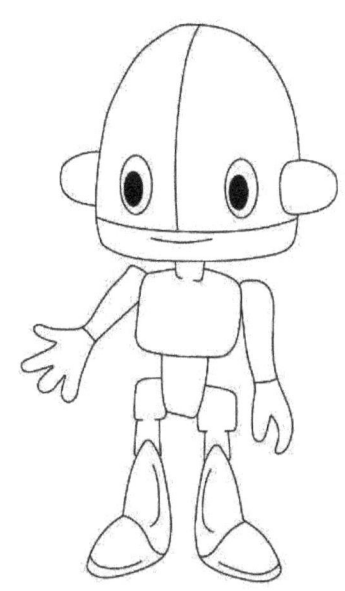

_____

_____

_____

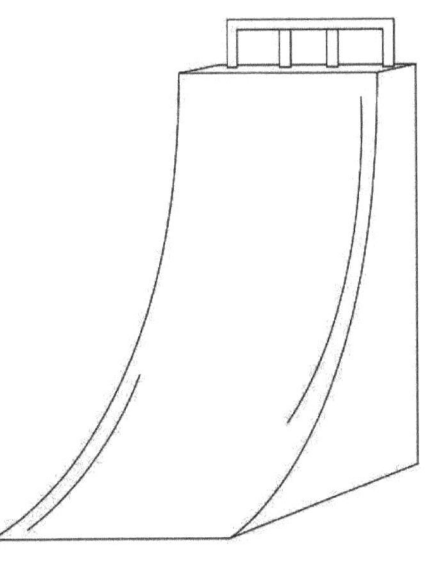

_____

_____

Directions: Say each word. Color each picture that starts with the letter Ss and is a noun. Cross (X) out each picture that does not begin with the letter or is not a noun. Use the box to draw a picture that starts with the letter and is a noun. Trace each letter at the bottom of the page.

Enrichment Activity

Directions: Look at the pictures and label the nouns only. Write the word that starts with the letter Ss and is a noun.

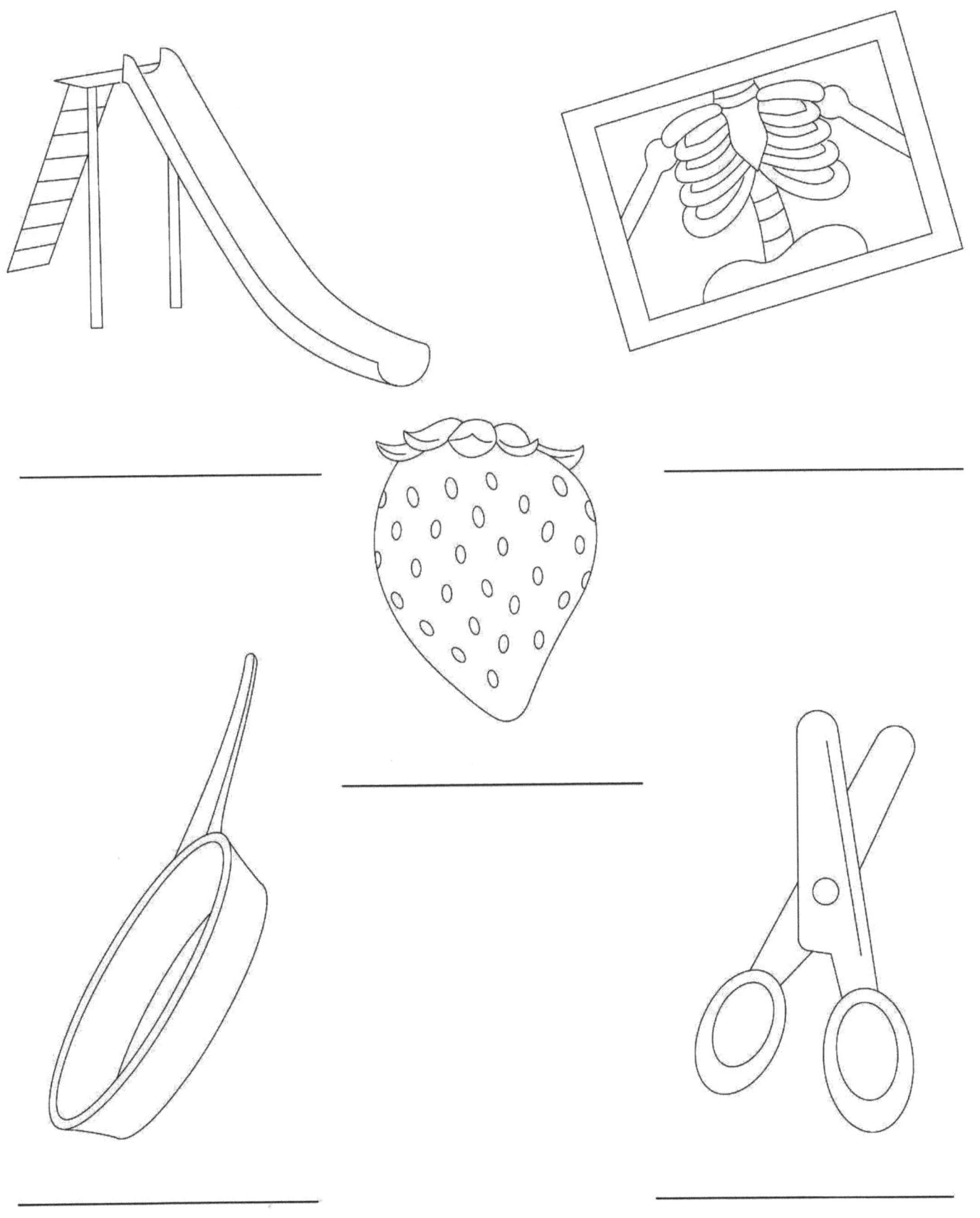

Directions: Say each word. Color each picture that starts with the letter Tt and is a noun. Cross (X) out each picture that does not begin with the letter or is not a noun. Use the box to draw a picture that starts with the letter and is a noun. Trace each letter at the bottom of the page.

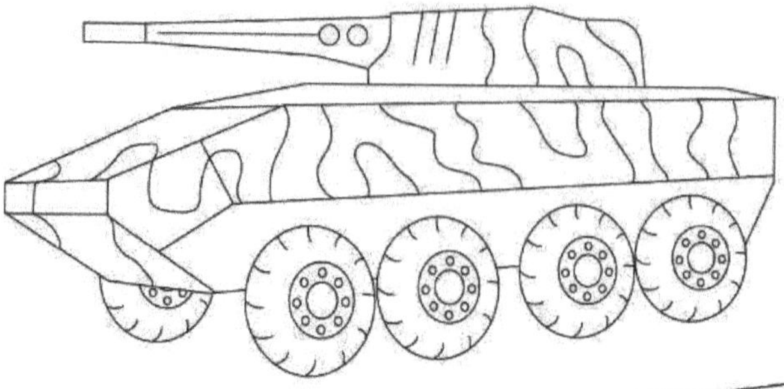

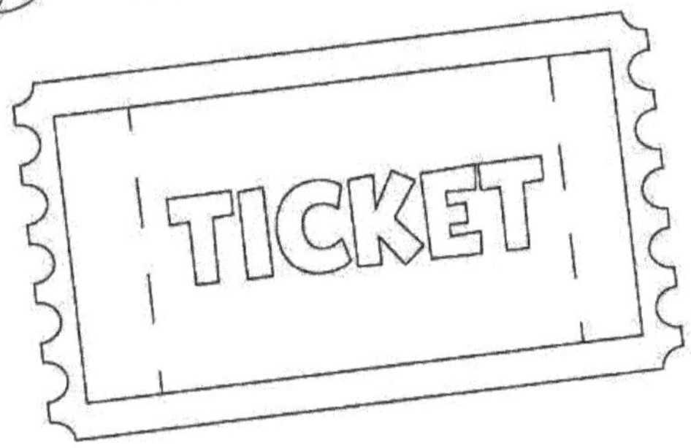

10 Tt

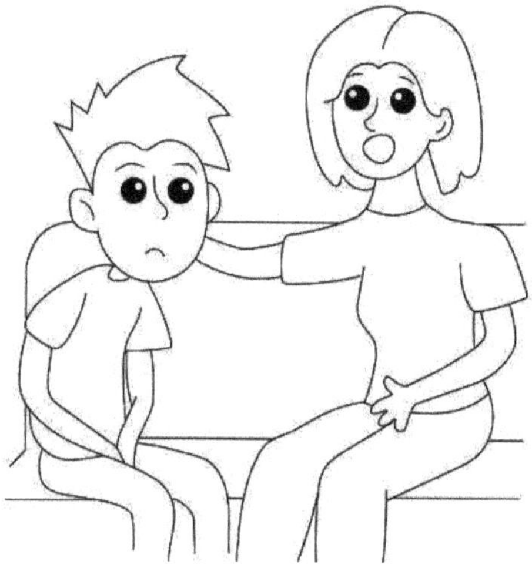

Enrichment Activity

Directions: Look at the pictures and label the nouns only. Write the word that starts with the letter Tt and is a noun.

_____   _____

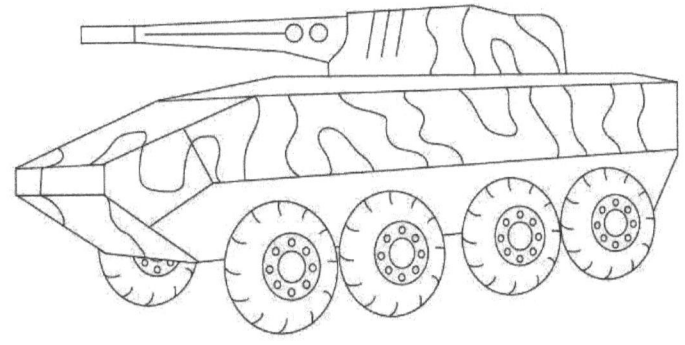

_____

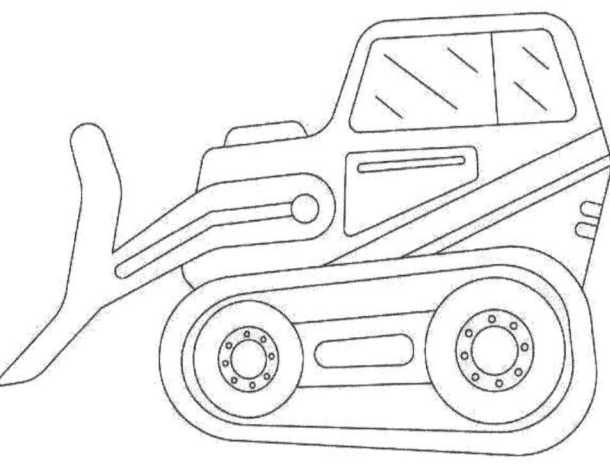

_____   _____

Directions: Say each word. Color each picture that starts with the letter Uu and is a noun. Cross (X) out each picture that does not begin with the letter or is not a noun. Use the box to draw a picture that starts with the letter and is a noun. Trace each letter at the bottom of the page.

Enrichment Activity

Directions: Look at the pictures and label the nouns only. Write the word that starts with the letter Uu and is a noun.

_____

_____

_____

UNIVERSITY

_____

_____

Directions: Say each word. Color each picture that starts with the letter Vv and is a noun. Cross (X) out each picture that does not begin with the letter or is not a noun. Use the box to draw a picture that starts with the letter and is a noun. Trace each letter at the bottom of the page.

Enrichment Activity

Directions: Look at the pictures and label the nouns only. Write the word that starts with the letter Vv and is a noun.

Directions: Say each word. Color each picture that starts with the letter Ww and is a noun. Cross (X) out each picture that does not begin with the letter or is not a noun. Use the box to draw a picture that starts with the letter and is a noun. Trace each letter at the bottom of the page.

Enrichment Activity

Directions: Look at the pictures and label the nouns only. Write the word that starts with the letter Ww and is a noun.

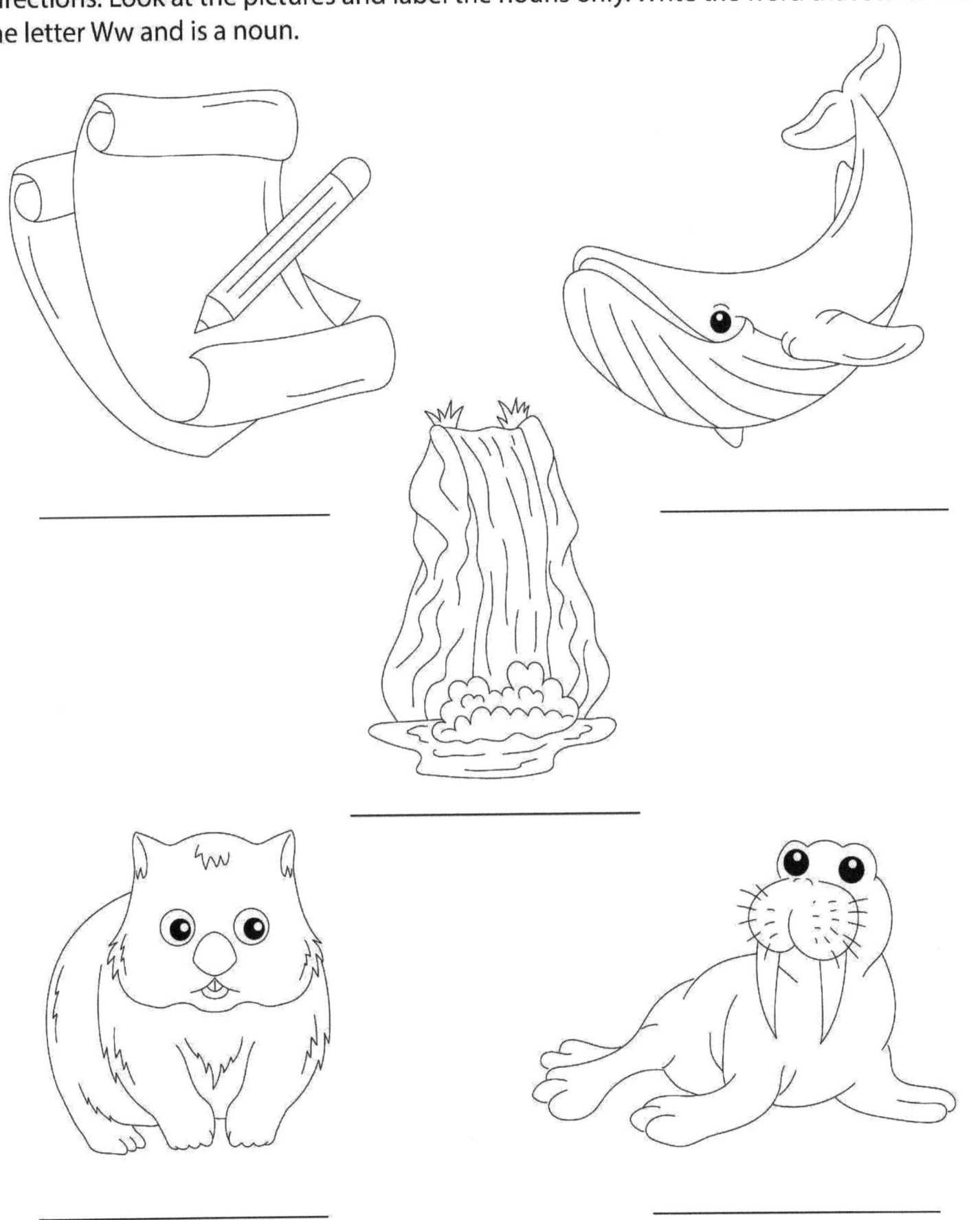

_____

_____

_____

_____

_____

Directions: Say each word. Color each picture that starts with the letter Xx and is a noun. Cross (X) out each picture that does not begin with the letter or is not a noun. Use the box to draw a picture that starts with the letter and is a noun. Trace each letter at the bottom of the page.

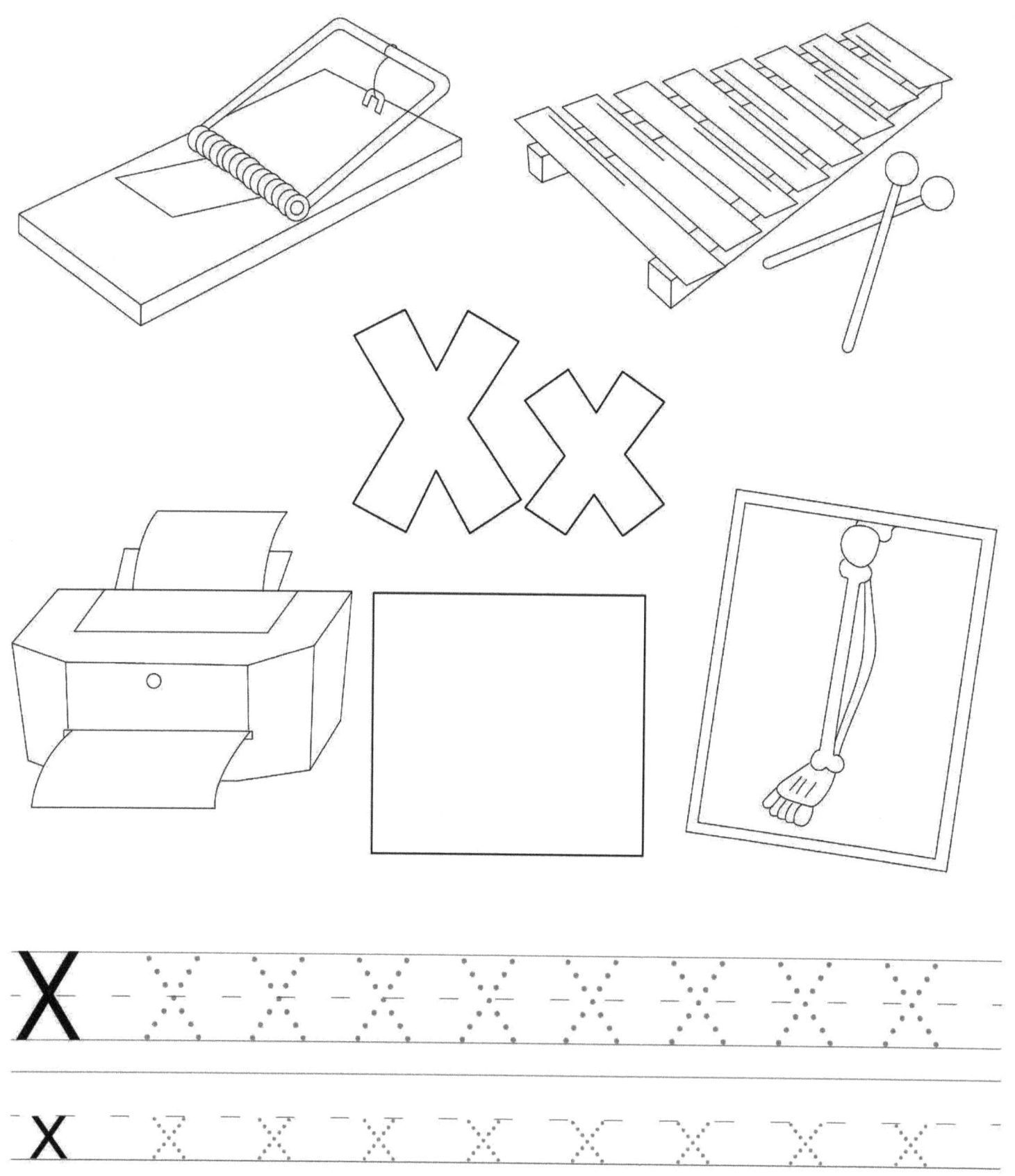

Enrichment Activity

Directions: Look at the pictures and label the nouns only. Write the word that starts with the letter Xx and is a noun.

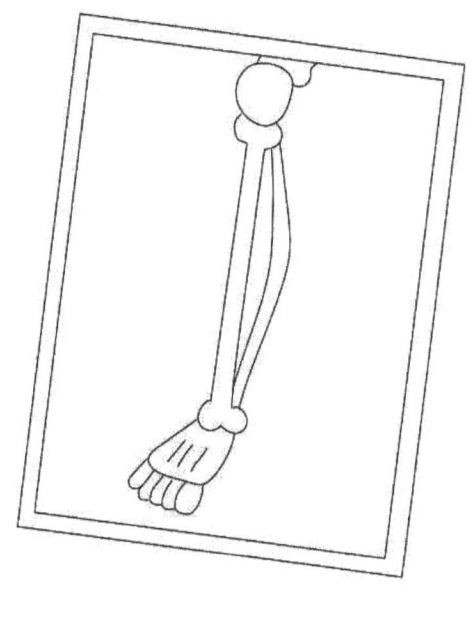

_____

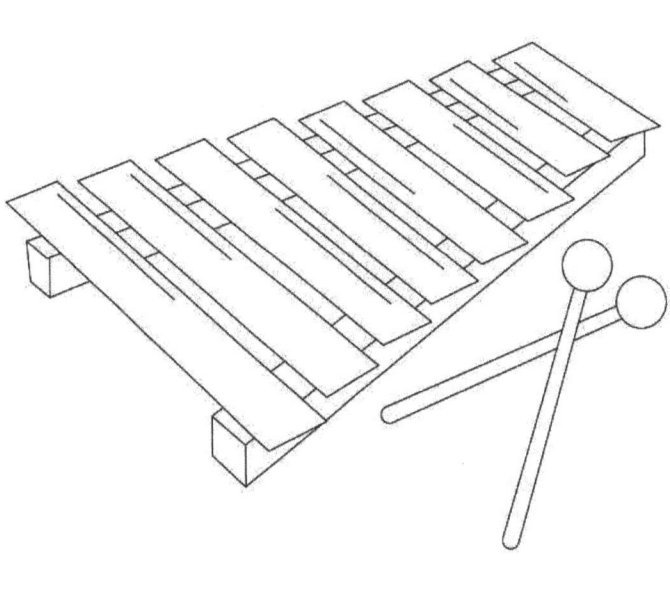

_____

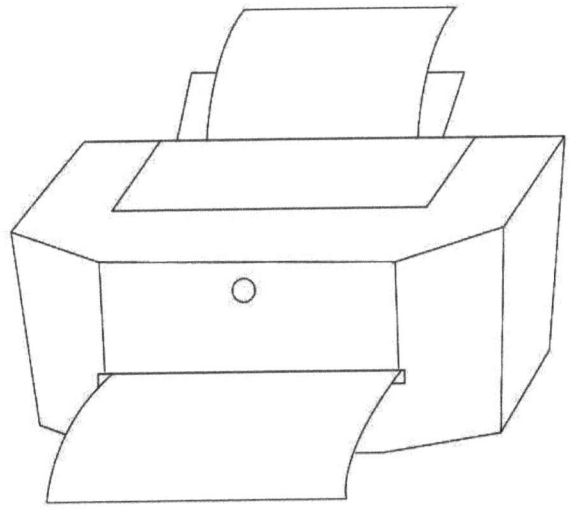

_____

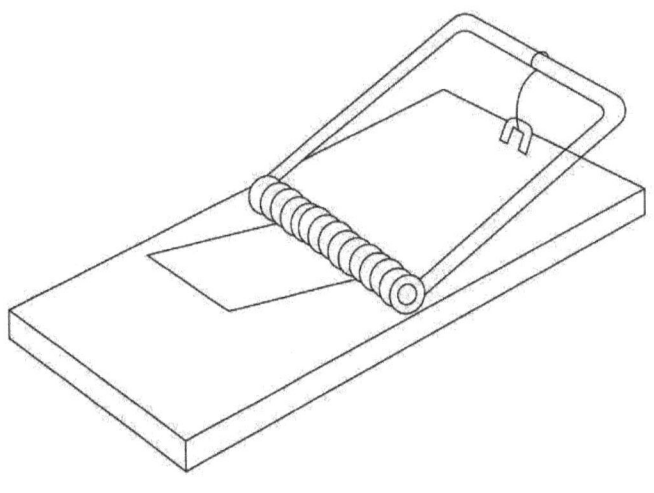

_____

Directions: Say each word. Color each picture that starts with the letter Yy and is a noun. Cross (X) out each picture that does not begin with the letter or is not a noun. Use the box to draw a picture that starts with the letter and is a noun. Trace each letter at the bottom of the page.

Yy

Yellow

Y ⋅Y⋅ ⋅Y⋅ ⋅Y⋅ ⋅Y⋅ ⋅Y⋅ ⋅Y⋅ ⋅Y⋅

y ⋅y⋅ ⋅y⋅ ⋅y⋅ ⋅y⋅ ⋅y⋅ ⋅y⋅ ⋅y⋅

Enrichment Activity

Directions: Look at the pictures and label the nouns only. Write the word that starts with the letter Yy and is a noun.

Directions: Say each word. Color each picture that starts with the letter Zz and is a noun. Cross (X) out each picture that does not begin with the letter or is not a noun. Use the box to draw a picture that starts with the letter and is a noun. Trace each letter at the bottom of the page.

Enrichment Activity

Directions: Look at the pictures and label the nouns only. Write the word that starts with the letter Zz and is a noun.

_____

_____

O

_____

_____

_____

Answer Documents

Letter of the Alphabet	Objects List
A	astronaut aquarium airplane ate award ask astrophysicist
B	bank island bridge boil cash blow bandage
C	cat crawl cardinal church school gum crying
D	daddy dance dig dessert dinner drive deer
E	elephant eagle eat elevator goose honey
F	frame foot orange fountain lemon fishing
G	grapes garden guitar goat grass gym
H	honey hippopotamus hay heart hill highway pinecone
I	cubes/blocks iron leaves island record
J	jacket jellyfish jar Jupiter jack jump dance
K	key stove kite knife kayak
L	ladder letter lemon/lime lunch luggage
M	mountain medicine milkshake meat mermaid nuts math
N	magazine book tissue nectarine napping notebook
O	ostrich owl ocean onion orange sign
P	pineapple popcorn box hop panther plant ring
Q	question marks quail quoll parrot tractor quilt
R	red paint rooster ramp run jeep robot
S	pan strawberry swing x-ray scissors slide
T	ten tank bulldozer talk ticket toad boy
U	ball unicorn umbrella utensils clothes university
V	violin volcano vegetables vase vacuum ballot box/vote
W	whale world weight walrus wombat write waterfall
X	x-ray xylophone xerox machine trap
Y	yak yacht carrot ruler yellow paint yo-yo yell
Z	zero zebra skunk zipper zookeeper

Alphabet/Noun Answer Key

Letter of the Alphabet	Nouns
A	astronaut aquarium airplane award astrophysicist
B	bank bridge bandage
C	cat cardinal church
D	daddy dessert dinner deer
E	elephant eagle elevator
F	frame foot fountain
G	grapes garden guitar goat grass gym
H	honey hippopotamus hay heart hill highway
I	iron island
J	jacket jellyfish jar Jupiter jug jack
K	key kite knife kayak
L	ladder letter lemon/lime lunch luggage
M	mountain medicine milkshake meat mermaid math
N	nectarine notebook
O	ostrich owl ocean onion orange
P	pineapple popcorn panther plant
Q	question marks quail quoll quilt
R	robot rooster ramp
S	strawberry swing scissors slide
T	ten tank ticket toad
U	unicorn umbrella utensils university
V	violin volcano vegetables vase vacuum
W	whale world weight walrus wombat waterfall
X	x-ray xylophone xerox machine
Y	yak yacht yo-yo
Z	zero zebra zipper zookeeper

Enrichment Answer Key

Letter of the Alphabet	Nouns
A	astronaut aquarium award astrophysicist
B	bank bridge bandage
C	cat cardinal church
D	daddy dessert dinner
E	elephant eagle elevator
F	foot fountain
G	garden guitar goat grass gym
H	honey hippopotamus hay hill
I	iron island
J	jacket jellyfish jar Jupiter jack
K	key kite knife kayak
L	ladder letter lemon/lime lunch luggage
M	mountain milkshake meat mermaid
N	notebook
O	ostrich owl ocean onion orange
P	pineapple popcorn panther plant
Q	question marks quail quoll
R	robot rooster ramp
S	strawberry scissors slide
T	tank ticket toad
U	unicorn umbrella university
V	violin volcano vegetables vase vacuum
W	whale walrus wombat waterfall
X	x-ray xylophone xerox machine
Y	yak yacht yo-yo
Z	zero zebra zipper zookeeper